ISBN: 978-1-7366471-0-3

Erica Stephens

Sullivan of the Sea

Illustrated by Lia Monguzzi

Sullivan of the sea
Sullivan of the sea
And a'hoy mate
A'hoy mate

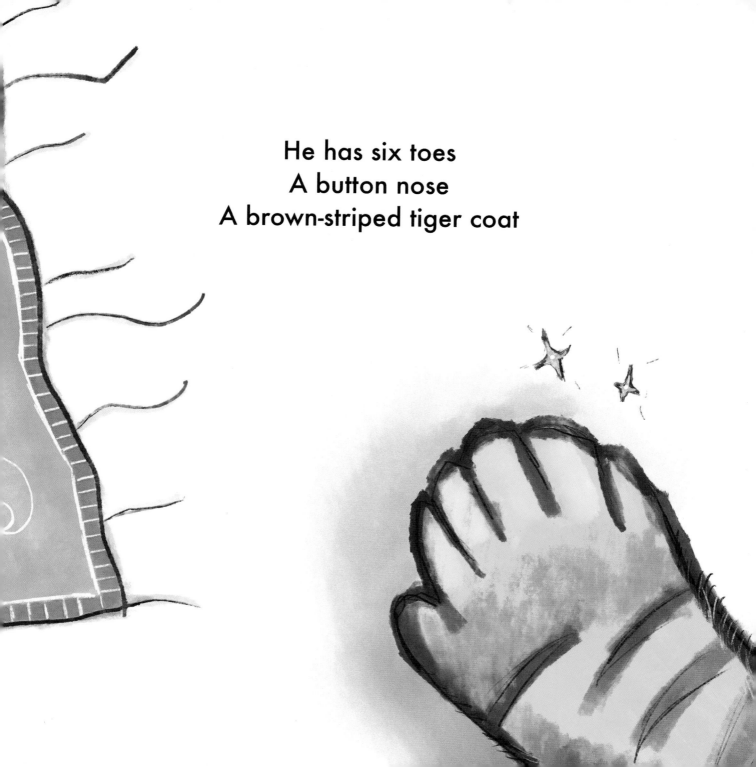

He has six toes
A button nose
A brown-striped tiger coat

He's a gentle soul

The best hunter we know

Sullivan of the sea
Sullivan of the sea

1893, born t'a peasant family
They loved him so, but had no gold
"Not anoth'r mouth to feed!"

So in the cold he wandered

And in the cold he slept...

...until his wee lungs cried for help
and his paws were made of ice

A pirate heard his cries
and thought "What a terr'ble fate!"

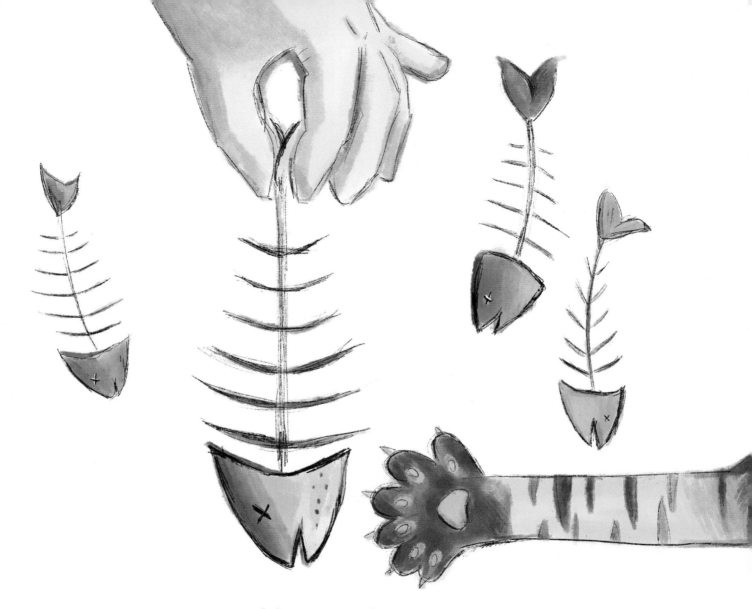

He scooped him up, fed'm scraps of trout
and made him his first mate!

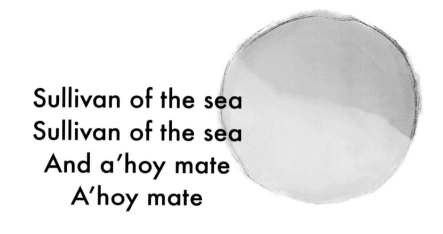

Sullivan of the sea
Sullivan of the sea
And a'hoy mate
A'hoy mate

They sail'd the ocean blue

They scavenged wrecks below

Sully played with mice, wore everything nice
ate like piggies, living a cat's best dream

They lived on the seas forev'r
as happy as could be
climbing ropes and sailing boats
Sullivan of the sea

Made in the USA
Coppell, TX
03 April 2021